To: Li
May [the Lord bless]
and keep you.
Min James
6-18-17 :)

"Mr.I"
-Selfishness, World-Worldly Systems, Satan-Adversary the Enemies we Face

James Roberts

authorHOUSE®

AuthorHouse™
1663 Liberty Drive
Bloomington, IN 47403
www.authorhouse.com
Phone: 1-800-839-8640

© 2009 James Roberts. All rights reserved.

No part of this book may be reproduced, stored in a retrieval system, or transmitted by any means without the written permission of the author.

First published by AuthorHouse   10/23/2009

ISBN: 978-1-4490-2496-3 (e)
ISBN: 978-1-4490-2495-6 (sc)

Library of Congress Control Number: 2009910633

Printed in the United States of America
Bloomington, Indiana

This book is printed on acid-free paper.

Table of Contents

Dedication vii
Foreword ix
Introduction. xi

Section One: Big Mr "I"- Selfishness
1. What is Selfishness... 1
2. Me, Myself and I 3
3. It's all about me Syndrome. 4
4. The commandment I give "Love"....................... 6
5. Renew your mind to "Love" 8
6. Mercy Mercy Mercy 9
7. Having to Prepare Ourselves............................. 11
Conclusion... 13

Section Two: World-Worldly Systems
1. Human Wisdom or Philosophy........................ 15
2. It a Mad Mad World. 17
3. Give me a Break. 18
4. Satan Place(World). 20
5. How to Overcome the World............................23
6. Mind Renewal..24
7. Faith in God. 26
8. Seek the Kingdom of God.................................28
9. Trust in God...30
10. Never go Back. 32
Conclusion: Standing with God. 34

Section Three: Satan-Adversary
1. Satan the Accuser..37
2. The Origin of Satan(Devil) 39
3. Bait of Satan...41

4. Works of Satan..43
5. "The Devil made me Do It"..............................45
6. An Angel of Light..47
7. The New Creation..49
8. Authority the Key...51
9. Spiritual Tactics..54
Conclusion..62

After Thoughts Part One....................................65
After Thoughts Part Two...................................69
Prayer for Salvation..72
God's Promises..73
Scriptures are taken from, the King James Version..73

Dedication

I like to dedicate this book to
my wonderful children
Brandon, Michael, and Vonessa
also Pastor Dale's children
Josiah, Judea, and Jahleel

A special thanks
to
Eunice Davis
for her expertise on
editing this book

Foreword

We are both very excited and Godly proud of Bro. James Roberts in such a way as this. In just a short time of him submitting to the ministry, we have been encourage as well as inspired by his maturity and commitment to the Lord. Bro. James is a very humble man and truly walks the walk that he talks about in the book. In the middle of a great faith trail; caused by an unforeseen accident, he had to believe GOD for restoration. The LORD began to use him as a pen of a ready writer to help others get the victory through their own personal trials. This book does just that, in a very practical way. There is much truth in every point given and as believers; we much continue to gain wisdom and knowledge by relevant experience. Therefore, it is imperative for each individual reader to take full advantage of every principle broken down from the heart of Bro. Roberts. In doing so, it will ensure victory from the common Enemy We Face. GOD Bless!

Pastor Dale and Lady Joan Hamilton

Introduction.

Selfishness, worldly systems, and Satan are enemies that will overtake believers to fall from the will of God. When you become a born again Christian, the power of heaven will back you up.(2Corinthians 5:17) states that "any man be in Christ, he is a new creature: old things are passed away, behold all things are become new." The true nature of man is his spirit, which becomes alive and hunger for the things that God has to offer.

This journey, " Let us then run with patience the race that is set before us"(Hebrews 12:1). There are enemies that lurk in darkness to take you away from your destiny and the purpose of God for your life. In this book, I will unlock some truths on these enemies and how to overcome their plans against you.

The big Mr."I"- selfishness. What is selfishness? Selfishness is seeking or concentrating on one's own advantage, pleasure, self gratification, or well being without regard for others. The Bible teaches us to love one another (Matthew 22:39) to defeat selfishness. When selfishness enters into one's heart, satisfaction of needs are accomplish by the manipulation of others for your gain only.

The world-worldly system is a way of operating, technical precept, beliefs, concepts, and attitudes which are govern by the wisdom of human philosophy. In (Romans 12:2)"be not conformed to this world." which mean, not allowing the world to fashion your way of thinking. The world is an enemy because it traps us into depending on the system, man's wisdom instead of God. Yes, as Christians we live in this world, but not apart of the worldly systems; a way of operating by man's wisdom. We are ambassadors for Christ(2Corinthians 5:20), which means, as Christians we are authorized representatives appointed by God for a special assignment; that is to represent heaven on this Earth or world and to serve others.

Lastly, Satan is our adversary, the devil(1Peter 5:8). Satan is the most lethal and in control of the others, big Mr."I" and the worldly systems. Satan is an enemy to God, and an enemy to you. Satan's objective is to get you out of the will of God for your life. In order for Satan to accomplish this, he will attack your faithfulness. Faithfulness for the believer is strong assurance to the promises of God. Satan is a defeated foe because of your commitment to God.

This book will give you guidance on how the enemy operates and how to overcome them. Victory for the believer. I will explain what the body of Christ is up against, Big Mr."I", worldly systems, Satan-adversary. Jesus came to destroy the works of the devil(1John 3:8) and enjoy life and have it in abundance, to the full, till it overflows(John10:10b amplified bible). We must be alert and keep our focus on things that are above (Colossians 3:2). A soldier on a battlefield will not overcome the enemy unless they know something about how the enemy operates. The enemy is a hostile force set out to kill you or take you prisoner. Spiritual warfare is like being on the battlefield. You must become familiar with your opponent to defeat them. This is what the book is about- to overcome your enemy and live a victorious lifestyle. Once the enemy is exposed, the advantage is ours to put the enemy under our feet and keep Him there. This book will help you get there.

Section I
"Big Mr. I" selfishness

1. What is Selfishness.

Selfishness is seeking or concentrating on one's own advantage, pleasure, or well being without regard for others. There is a story in the Bible about "The rich young ruler" (Matthew 19:16-22). I guess you're wondering what this story has to do with being selfish. First, the rich ruler asked Jesus a question, "what must I do to have eternal life?"(Matthew 19:16). Now Jesus pointed out to keep the commandments that God gave in Moses time(v.18-19). The rich ruler acknowledged that he was obedient. The point I want to express here about selfishness is in verses 21 "if thou be perfect, go and sell what thou hast, and give to the poor......" Jesus made it clear to the rich ruler to sell everything he had and give it to the poor.

The rich ruler was amazed at what Jesus said. The Bible didn't give an account on how the ruler became rich, but he went away from Jesus feeling sorrow because he didn't want to give up his possessions. His heart was on the things he accumulated, if not, he would have done what

Jesus told him to do. Selfishness comes from within the heart. You focus on fulfilling a gratification which brings pleasure within yourself which brings completeness to your well being.

When being selfish, manipulation of others manifest in order to meet or gain acceptance for selfish needs. Don't get me wrong here, there are times when selfishness has it roles. Selfishness becomes an enemy by using people to get what you want, regardless of how the other person feels. As long as your needs are met, that's what counts.

2. Me, Myself and I

Let's look at a story in the Bible of someone with this attitude of me, myself and I.(Isaiah 14:12-14)*"How art thou fallen from heaven, O Lucifer, son of the morning! how art thou cut down to the ground, which did weaken the nations! For thou has said in thine heart, " I will ascend into the heaven, I will exalt my throne above the stars of God. I will sit also upon the mount of the congregation, in the sides of the north: I will ascend above the heights of the clouds. I will be like the most High.* Lucifer purposed in his heart to be better than God. What motived this behavior? pride.

Pride is a trait of someone who is selfish, because the person feels they are better than others. The Bible calls pride a "proud look". (Proverbs 6:17). Selfishness brings distorted thoughts to oneself, example, "I'm better than you", "it doesn't matter how you feel", and it's all about me not you" etc. When you think this way, it becomes a lifestyle looking out for number one(me). "For as a man thinks in his heart , so is he" (Proverbs 23:7a). You think selfish thoughts, then you become selfish; not understanding the regards of others.

Satan knew in his heart that if he could become greater or mightier than God, that would turn all the focus and attention to him. Selfishness is attention, gain, and acceptance for your glory only. Selfishness is that act of placing one's own needs or desires above the needs or desires of others. Let's keep in mind that God created you to serve others; but, if you're not submitted to do so, you'll began to serve yourself.

3. It's all about me Syndrome.

People have an agenda of being successful or unsuccessful when it comes to daily living. What brings out selfishness is when the individual sees opportunity that only satisfies ego for self. In other words,"It's all about me!" The story of the prodigal son (Luke 15:11-16) has this characteristic. First the son wanted what belonged to him, which was acceptable, but his intentions or motives were wrong. Giving the account of the substance; it made him feel important and powerful. When others are manipulated for your gain, a sense of being in control is apparent.

Secondly, acting on impulses instead of planning, he went on a journey living a life of wastefulness just to be accepted by others. He was overly concerned with his own desires and needs at the expense of others. He became self centered. It's hard work to be selfish, because if a certain need isn't met, than you go out of the way to satisfy that need, which I call selfish ambition or it's all about me syndrome.

Unselfish ambition for the believer is good because your focus is on the needs and love for others. Selfishness, on the other hand, will lead you down the road of destruction. That's what happened to the prodigal son. He partied away his substances and ended up in the hog pin. Where do you stand? Loving and caring or it's about me syndrome? Now, since selfishness has been exposed, which is only the tip of the iceberg, let's look at some ways to defeat this enemy and have victory over selfish behavior. I want to give some practical ways for success. Don't allow the enemy, (Satan), access over your well being in Christ. The only way Satan can attack you is with ideals, thoughts, and suggestions. That's why the Bible teaches us to pull down strongholds and bring every thought in the obedience of Christ.(2 Corinthians 10:4-5).

4. The commandment I give "Love"

"Jesus said unto him, Thou shalt love the Lord thy God with all thy heart and with all thou soul, and with all thy mind. This is the first and great commandment and the second is like unto it, Thou shalt love thy neighbor......"(Matthew 22:37-39). Love is the key, which will remove your attention from being selfish and having the consideration of serving others. Jesus was a master at showing compassion to people. Love will leave you open to receive blessings from God when meeting the needs of others. Therefore, love will defeat the enemy of selfishness, and now your concentration is on the people that are hurting for love. Joy will come to your spirit knowing that you helped someone's needs to be met. When you are involved in the affairs of others, your maturity for compassion is stable.

The nature of God is love(1John 4:8) a strong affection for humankind. We as believer must demonstrate this kind of love; that will bring hope to someone hurting or in need. Selfishness is the enemy and the way to conquer it is by displaying love and taking our attention from self to serving others. Everything in the kingdom of God operates by faith. Faith works to produce love and brings out the fruit thereof.(Galatians 5:22). When love is deep rooted in the heart(spirit), it will produce the God kind of love. Expressing love will overcome selfishness, but love will become dormant where selfishness rules. When we meet people's physical needs first, God will open the door to address their spiritual needs.

5. Renew your mind to "Love"

You must bring to your attention a different mind set for meeting other people's needs. As mentioned earlier, you must get your mind from self to loving others. When you are born-again, your spirit becomes alive in Christ. The mind and soul basically stay the same. In (Romans 12:1-2) enlighten the believer to renew their mind. You must spend time in the Word to begin the process of renewing the mind. Worldly systems was your way of thinking before you were born again. Therefore the mind must be renewed. A way to renew your mind is to meditate on the Word of God. (Joshua 1:8). Meditating helps to renew our mind. To meditate means to mutter over and over until the scripture become a normal way of living or thinking. Once you develop a habit of reading the Bible, study, prayer, and listening to tapes, your mind will become renewed. When renewing the mind, you are replacing the worldly way of thinking with the way God thinks, which is through his Word.

Love will come when you meet the physical needs of others. Love will be an important role when it comes to meeting people's spiritual needs as well. The enemy of self is defeated when godly love is sown. Remember, God will not violate your will. To renew your mind is a matter of choice. To overcome selfishness, you must be willing to bring yourself to a state of having an interest or concern for others.

6. Mercy Mercy Mercy

Mercy is a blessing that is an act of divine favor or compassionate treatment of those in distress. Throughout the Bible, Jesus was very compassionate. He healed the sick, cast out demons, and many other miracles. This is the example that the believers should have compassion too. (John 13:15) There are times when self preservation has it roles, such as to satisfy hunger, thirst, protection, and health. Obsessively concentrating on selfish behavior weakens your true nature, limiting your ability to effectively serve others.

Showing mercy brings hope to the hearts of people that have fallen on hard times. Giving to other people's needs will come back to you. It's a principle in the Bible called sowing and reaping. (Galatians 6:7). You sow love, then love is the harvest that comes back to you. We as believers must always show mercy, love, thoughtfulness and sympathy for others.

Let's look in the Bible at someone having compassion and mercy. It's a familiar story about the "Good Samaritan" found in (Luke 10:25-37). There was a traveler going to a certain town. On the way he was robbed, and left on the side of the road to die. Two men came down the road, saw him lying there, but went on their way without attending to the wounded man. Having no compassion or mercy is a selfish act, because you don't want to get involved in other people's affairs or the affairs of people in distress.

On the other hand, a man is riding down the road, see's the wounded man; however, mercy and compassion was in this man's heart. The man made sure the wounded man was comfortable by tending to his wounds. He then went to the inn with the man told the innkeeper to take care of him and paid for his stay. This man had a sympathetic consciousness of this traveler's distress, having a desire to alleviate the traveler's wounded spirit. This is love at it's best because the man was focused on someone else. He interrupted his plans for a moment and cared for a complete stranger. As believers, we need to have that same caring and loving spirit. Satan hates acts of kindness, because of the rewards or blessing received from God for those acts. Selfishness dries up sympathy for others.

7. Having to Prepare Ourselves.

In order to defeat the enemy, preparation for a defense is vital for victory. Believers are not ignorant of Satan's devices(2Corinthians 2:11). Awareness of selfish traits, which is one of Satan devices, can be an avenue towards developing compassion for others. Your attitude prepares you to give of yourself, because of the choices that are made. God will not violate your will, but is displeased when you only focus and concentrate on yourself. Prepare yourself with God's words, which are knowledge, so that the enemy will not get a hold of you. Start looking for God's will in your life. Safe guard the things you value, pay strict attention to the Holy Spirit. When you have compassion it comes from within your spirit. It's the Holy Spirit that's leading you away from selfishness and causing a deep urge to serve others that are afflicted, experiencing hardship, and feeling heartbroken.

Preparation, awareness, and safeguards are an advantage for a successful victory over selfish thoughts. Bring to reality the true love that God want us to possess. (Matthew22:37-39) The good Samaritan displayed great compassion and understood the need that would lead to a blessing from Heaven. Giving the account that this enemy will divert you from being compassionate and only seek selfish gain and glory. It was instructed by *Jesus* to *preach the gospel to the poor, heal the brokenhearted, preach deliverance to the captive, recovering* sight to the blind, and *set at liberty them that are bruised.*(Luke 4:18). These instructions will only come when compassion for others is placed on your heart. Selfishness will not reap compassion; but, compassion reaps love. Love will bring you out or conquer selfish behavior and prepare you with a caring and willing spirit that brings hope to others.

Let's keep in mind that we are going to be bombarded with thoughts, ideas, and suggestions from the enemy to discourage you from the will of God concerning the needs of others. Jesus says "walk in love" (Ephesians 5:2). Put yourself in position with God to receive and focus on what is needed to care. Keep in mind that when caring for others, you will not lack(Proverbs 28:27) in your life . Be on the lookout and sustain that which is godly and brings praises to your spirit.

Preparation is the key for overcoming selfishness, because it enlightens on providing ways of giving yourself to someone that is in need. If you want harmony and stability in life, then get involved with loving and caring for others. Total satisfaction evolves maturity in the spirit, soul, and body. When you are in God's will-and Jesus left us an example to follow-power and compassion become a lifestyle. Surrendering selfish motives totally equips you with strength to give of yourself. The body of Christ has to be strong and set the tone so that people are healed in every area of their lives. Being unselfish isn't easy. The flesh and it's way of thinking, will only be concerned with you only. I call it the battle of the mind. The choice is yours to make.

Conclusion.

The big "Mr. I" is selfish behavior that causes love to be dormant. Remember selfishness is seeking or concentrating on one's own advantage, pleasure, or well being without regard for others. It's all about me syndrome brings glory to self. Let's understand that it is alright to be selfish when it comes to sustaining life (ex. hunger, thirst, and air etc.); but, if it becomes an obsession to the point of seeking selfish ways and having no concerns for others, then it becomes an enemy. You have no conscience when you ignore those who are hurting for love and acceptance. Jesus shuns this type of behavior because this wasn't the example he left us to follow.

Once you begin to adjust your attitude for others, the rewards will overwhelm the inner man within(Spirit). Preparation to fight "Big Mr, I"-selfishness, you must know who you are in Christ to claim the victory. Let me encourage you to keep a level head when helping those in need. Adjust your plans, see to the need, and move on. That's what the good Samaritan did. Watch out for those who will take kindness for granted. You may help them once, but if they keep coming back, then be firm with love and understanding and let that individual know that the help is no longer available. The Holy Spirit will warn of this kind of deception. That's why it is important to listen to your inner voice. Keep love in your heart, be aware of the needs of others, and honor the commandment(Matthew

22:37-39). This brings peace and joy to the spirit and soul. Be strong in the Lord and in the power of His might (Ephesian 6:10) to fight the enemy of selfishness. When you go the extra mile and give of yourself, God notices it as a sacrifice to Him. God created us to be a blessing to others. Christians need to flow in the Spirit of love; being mindful of those that are hurting. There are many ways to meet people's needs: giving things, a word of encouragement, compliments, doing a service, and so much more. Showing love constantly and the way we treat one another is important to God. Guard your love walk; if not the enemy will divert you into another dimension that causes unloving behavior and selfishness to take root. Anywhere you see the spirit of "Big Mr. I" you see the spirit of Satan(Isaiah14:13-14). Love is giving unselfishly. Keeping that in mind will bring forth completeness of heart, victory over selfishness, and honor to God. God gave His best, His only begotten son Jesus, (John3:16). Therefore we as Christians need to give our best.

Section II
World-World Systems

1. Human Wisdom or Philosophy.

The worldly systems, what is it? A system that pursues the wisdom of men, basic beliefs, concepts, man's attitudes of individuals or groups. The most obvious is a system that totally opposes the kingdom of God or the Godly way of living. The world systems keep you in bondage and fear. It's in the news all the time. Job layoff, crime of all kind, stock market blues and bank collapse, only naming a few. People are looking for ways of comfort and finding none. Living this way keeps you on the edge, whether success will come to be or you experience failure of your dreams. When you allow the worldly system to govern your lifestyle, it becomes an enemy, because you are putting your trust in man's wisdom and not trusting God. The Bible makes it clear not to love the world (1John 2:15). Three things occur when living in the world(1John 2:16): 1. lust of the flesh; 2. lust of the eyes; and 3. pride of life. Could it be that the spirit is willing but the flesh is weak(Matthew 26:41) because of the influence that the worldly system has on society.

Many people are depending on human reasoning for their welfare. Employment, education, transportation and housing are necessary. If not careful in methods of attaining these things could lead to destruction. Worldly systems are always changing , and people feel they have a moral duty to abide by these changes. Changes are good, but when you struggle to meet these changes, that could cause unstable personalities. Things like depression, drug abuse, crime, vulnerability, weakness, and spiritual loss.

2. It a Mad Mad World.

Anxiety, worry, emptiness, and restlessness, from the news media shows the shape that this world is in. Hurting people looking for a way out and finding none. Remember the hurricanes that hit the Texas and Louisiana coast. The government was rated low in responding to the people's needs. Still, this day, people are suffering and looking for hope.

Now, I did mention that the worldly system is an enemy and the reason why is because it is unstable. A mind fixated on the worldly systems and the flesh is what leads to stress, trouble, emptiness, and unrest; especially of the mind. Worldly systems have their own way of settling affairs (man wisdom). When you are living worldly, then that compromises the true state of victorious living. Depending on the worldly systems about your circumstances will keep you wondering what's going to happen next. You solve one situation by man wisdom and something else pops up causing another stress. What are you going to do to keep a stress free life? When you are born-again and don't renew your mind, you are setting yourself up for failure because you choose to live by the standards of the worldly systems. Today it's about self preservation. What I'm going to do for survival? Selfishness is based on worldly system habits. I have to look out for me. It doesn't matter what you think, and manipulating others to seek your own selfish desires. A person that's not born-again of Jesus, operates by this system(worldly).

3. Give me a Break.

Have you heard the old adage of "give me a break," "why are things happening to me?" and "I take one step forward to take two steps backwards" and many more cliché. The system of the world isn't fair. When you think your job is secure, your boss comes and says they are downsizing and they have to let you go. Your bank account is wiped out because of identity theft. The doctor says you have an incurable disease. As Christians, we have to make a choice which system to live by, worldly systems or the kingdom of God system. Adjustments are constantly made in the world system, keeping you guessing about your well being. Like the stock market up one day or down the next day. This is not how God want his children to live. III John 2 states, "beloved, I wish above all things that thou mayest prosper and be in health, even as thy soul prosper". God wants us to be made whole in every area of our life. The worldly system is designed to keep you in fear. It keeps you on the edge and helpless. Bad things do happen to good people, but it's how you respond to the situation that determines success or failure. Jesus was a master of operating in the kingdom of God system. The scribes and pharisees were master operating in the worldly systems, because of rules that they made. If you give your attention to the worldly systems wisdom, then your desires will depend on the standards of what the world has to offer. When you depend on doing things the world system way, then you're seeking man wisdom instead of God. You react to the environment that surrounds your way of living and making decisions based on your surroundings.

Jesus made decisions daily, kept his spirit tuned in to God the father, so that the world would know of his character. Jesus wasn't moved by the worldly systems because of what the world represented. Sin and death is of the world, truth and eternal life are of the kingdom of God. The worldly system isn't a place for the believer to operate in. It will lead to doubt, faith being compromised, and eventually leading you away from the will of God towards spiritual death. The Bible says: "To be strong in the Lord and in the power of his might".(Ephesians 6:10). If you are not deep rooted, the cares of this world will enter into your spirit and cause you to become unstable. Remember, the world system is designed to keep you guessing. That's why you are unstable, because you don't know which direction to take. If you want God's best, then deny self, remove your ways from worldly system way of living, and totally surrender and commit to God's way of living.

4. Satan Place(World).

When the war in heaven took place Satan and his fallen angels was cast into the Earth(Revelation 12:9). Satan is known for accusing Christians, and the worldly system is his stomping ground. Therefore Satan want to divert your attention on how the worldly system operates, to keep you from receiving God's best for your life. In (Matthew 6:33a) "but seek ye first the kingdom of God, and his righteousness......" but Satan will target your mind to seek the worldly system way of living. The worldly system is based in selfishness and Satan is the author of selfishness(Isaiah14:12-14). Satan is the god of this world and he is in the mist of destroying the world. Satan wants to steal, kill, and destroy you(John10:10a). Satan wants to steal the word from the heart, destroy your spiritual foundation and dreams, and take you out of the equation. Satan wants to kill you. The world is in turmoil because of Satan and he is not letting up.

For the Christian this is the battle we face daily and we must be able to handle the pressures of the world. If not, then Satan will have a grip on you that will cause stress to be apart of your way of living. Suggestions, ideals, and thoughts are weapons Satan uses to overcome your way of thinking. Today you can see his weapons in action. Same sex marriages, abortions, pornography, wars, occults, and many more. These are all distractions from the truth. Freedom is truth in the word of God(John 8:32) and

Satan wants to distract you from the truth. Truth is the kingdom of God's way of living; not by worldly system standards. The worldly system is an enemy because of the hardship it releases on individuals. Trying to keep up with the "Jones'," but going broke, unfulfilled, and stress out. Many Christians are in this dilemma, not focused in faith, but allowing circumstances to dictate their lives. If circumstances are a way of engaging your standard of living, then you are not trusting God. You are trusting yourself for deliverance and solving the problem. Usually it's not the best solution,but a temporary fix. Then something else occurs and the process starts all over again. This is how the worldly system operates with no peace of mind. Always on the level that keeps you in suspense. Why? Satan doesn't want you to be successful but confused, doubtful, and a lack of confidence is what he wants to put in your mind. Making you believe that there is no way out or no hope. Depression, fear, and doubt means for the believer, that they have allowed the worldly systems to defeat them. Looking at their circumstances instead of flowing in the spirit, brings on this defeated mentality. The way to overcome this defeated mentality is by policing your thoughts on life. If you don't confess to negative thoughts they will not be born. On the other hand, your confessing to negative thoughts will bring them alive. We are to bring into captivity every thought to the obedience of Christ.(2 Corinthians 4:6).

Remember thoughts, ideals, and suggestions are what Satan uses to move you from the will of God. When you compromise your faith in God, then you succumb to what the worldly systems offer, which is unstableness. Satan has the worldly system just where he wants it. People seeking their own way of problem solving. Giving attention to man's philosophy, not the wise counsel of God. Putting on fronts and deceiving others that everything is all right, but in reality things are in a state of utter confusion and chaos. We have to realize that the worldly system is an enemy to the body of Christ, and we have to overcome this system with the authority that Christ gave us.

5. How to Overcome the World.

The worldly systems are design to get your focus on your circumstances and depending on men philosophy for the answer or a way out. Satan control this system and his plan is to get you out of the will of God. Therefore let's look at five ways to be victorious over this system.

1. Mind Renewal.
2. Faith in God.
3. Seek the Kingdom of God.
4. Trust in God.
5. Never go Back.

We must not be defeated, because of how the world handles situations. "For everyone born of God overcomes the world. This is the victory that has overcome the world even our faith"(1 John 5:4niv). Jesus made it clear for the believer not to love the world. (1 John 2:15) What is in the worldly system that isn't safe for the spirit of man? The reason being is the conflict between flesh and spirit. Let me explain in detail the five ways that will bring success and victory to your Christians walk.

6. Mind Renewal.

Renewing the mind is vital for the new born Christian. When you become a born-again Christian, old things are passed away and new things become new(2 Corinthians 5:17). It's like God took his heavenly eraser and erased everything you ever did, and recorded your name in the Lamb Book of Life (Revelation 21:27) so that you can begin a new life in the spirit. When you are born-again, the inner man (spirit) is energized and made perfect with God, but your body and soul remain the same. Your soul is made up of your mind, emotions, will, and intellect and must be renewed in the things of God, to battle with the worldly systems. How do you renew your mind?

Let's look at(Romans 12:1-2) a very familiar passage of scripture, verse (2) is where I want to put emphasis. "Do not be conformed to this world(this age)[fashioned after and adapted to its external, superficial customs] but be transformed (change) by the [entire] renewal of your mind[by it new ideals and it new attitude] so that you may prove [for yourselves] what is the good and acceptable and perfect[in His sight for you. (Amplified Bible).

You begin to renew your mind by focusing on the things of God. When you were in the world you were brainwashed. Renewing your mind is a way of reprogramming the mind for victorious living. Reading your Bible daily, prayer, going to church, studying the Bible, and hearing the word of God, also seeing to the needs of others are ways of renewing your mind. Guarding your thought life is a way of mind renewal. Replacing negative thoughts with positive thoughts will change the way you think about your circumstances. Satan will attack you through the mind with ideals, thoughts, and suggestions, and if you bite the bait, you're hooked. See (2 Corinthains10:4-5) on how to control your thought life.

Renewing your mind is an on going process that will not happen overnight. Feeding yourself with the Word of God will help the mind to gravitate to God's way of living and thinking. You must have a desire to serve God, to bring your body and soul to subjection for faithfulness. Once your mind is renewed, you begin to recognize the true nature of God, which is love(1John 4:8).

7. Faith in God.

Hebrews 11:1 "Now faith is the substance of things hoped for, the evidence of things not seen". One of the attributes of a Christian is having faith. Faith is acting on the Word of God and what you believe. Coming out of the worldly systems is going to require you to use faith. You have to develop your faith in order to be successful and victorious over the things of this world. How do you develop your faith? Hearing God's word will develop your faith. "So then faith comes by hearing and hearing by the the Word of God"(Romans 10:17). Exercising your faith will develop your faith. No word no faith. We need faith to win battles. To overcome this worldly system is going to take faith for the victory(1John 5:4). Faith comes where the will of God is known.

"For we walk by faith, not by sight"(2 Corinthians 5:7). Walking by faith is acting on what you believe without the manifestation of the thing. Walking by sight is allowing your natural senses (sight, hearing, taste, touch, smell) to govern what you believe. I must see it first before I believe is often expressed when you allow your senses to take over. Let me give you an example. You look at your bank account and it is in the red. Now the word of God says wealth and riches shall be in his house (Psalms 112:3). You have a decision to make, believe what the word of God says about the situation and stand on that promise or choose to believe with your senses in reference to your bank account.

Standing on God's promises and not wavering will change your circumstances This is how we defeat this enemy, the worldly systems.

Worldly systems will keep you down for the count. "Be strong in the Lord and in the power of his might" (Ephesian6:10), taking the shield of faith to quench the darts that the worldly systems throw at you, and get up. Be more of a conqueror. Knockout the worldly systems and claim victory. Satan don't like being defeated. He will come at you again and again to put you under a stressful situation, to get your mind on your circumstances, instead of the things of God. Remember we are not ignorant of Satan's devices(2Corinthains 2:11). We can stop Satan dead in his tracks, by confessing God's word and using faith over circumstances. Life and death is in the power of the tongue(Proverbs18:21). Calling those things which be not as though there were (faith in action) is speaking life and victory over this world. It very important for Christians to have faith in God or the God kind of faith to overcome the stronghold of the worldly systems. Faith gives you that confidence that God will fight the battle and we are to hold our peace. We have at our disposal all what God offers. What we have to do is link up with that source, which is our faith. Without faith it is impossible to please God(Hebrews 11:6). With faith mountains can be moved.(Mark11:23)

8. Seek the Kingdom of God.

What is the kingdom of God? Being in conscious and constant communication, and knowledge of God. The kingdom of God is doing things that line up with God's word. We are bringing Him into the picture, obeying by seeking Him first (Matthew 6:33). When we do that we create the opportunity to put some interesting dynamics into action that will facilitate overcoming this worldly system. To have the right kind of fellowship and relationship with God, we have to be aware of the reality that we are always in His presence. He is " a God near at hand." God has promised never to leave or forsake us (Hebrews 13:5) and since we are the Temple where His spirit dwells(1Corinthians 3:16), God is constantly with us. Remember to seek God first in matters that bring wisdom and understanding in spiritual affairs. There's nothing that God can't do; but, if your heart is hardened, then you limit God on what is available to you. When you seek the kingdom of God, your attention is on pleasing Him, and taking a stand on who you are in Christ. The focus of Satan is to adjust your thinking away from the things of God to what's going on around you. Just like the bank account scenario. Satan will draw your attention to the balance and keep your mind on it constantly. keeping your thoughts from the promise of God, which is that wealth and riches shall be in his house(Psalms 112:3). Seeking the kingdom assures the Christian that God will drop a plan in their spirit to remove that negative bank account to an account that will overflow.

We live in a day of increasing wickedness, promotion of the most vile kind of sins. Our society is saturated with addiction of pleasure, profit, and power. The worldly system is based on selfish motives. Seeking the kingdom of God system is based in love. Always realize how important it is to stand on God's word when it comes to fighting the battle that Satan tries to put on us. The Bible says "Yet in all these things we are more than conquerors through Him who loved us". (Romans 8:37) meaning we are winners. We are well able to bring victory to any situation in our lives. Put the armor of God on (Ephesians 6:11) and the worldly system becomes useless. Our faith also overcomes the world(1John 5:4) and not to love the world (1John 2:15) will bring stability in our Christian lifestyle. God's way is the only way to go through unstable times and come out the victor, not the victim.

9. Trust in God.

Trusting God means to rely on, lean on, and depend on God. It's like a newborn infant baby. When the baby comes through the birth canal, the baby automatically begins to trust the mother and that bonding take place. It's because the baby knows the mother is there to take care of them. That's how God is, taking care of His children, because He loves them and will nurture them.

At the circus, the trapeze artists are swinging back and forth high in the air. One of artists begins a routine of acrobatic flips. Now the one that is doing the flips must trust and rely on the other artist to catch him. The other trapeze artist stretches out his hands and catches the other artist and both swing back to the platform. A trust must be developed between both artists. On the other hand if the trapeze artist remove his hands, fails to catch the artist and he falls to the safety net, then that trust is broken. That's what sin is to God, a trust breaker and being separated from God. Webster defines trust as: a charge or duty imposed in faith or as a condition of some relationship: something committed or entrusted to one to be used or cared for in the interest of another. The Bible say, to trust in God with all your heart and having confidence in your spirit that God is on your side in every situation. (See Proverbs 3:5-6). Trust brings us to that level of faith that produces good results over worldly negative decisions. God is our refuge and strength; a very present help in trouble(Psalms

46:1). Coming to a point that the cares of this world are pressuring you and setting you up for failure or having no way out of the dilemma, but trusting God will be your source in any situation and new beginning. Satan will put fear in your heart that you are going under. Fear is negative worry about what's going on in your life, God has not given us the spirit of fear, but of power, and of love and of a sound mind(2 Timothy1:7). Also if you are troubled in your heart trust in God. (John 14:1).

We must trust in the Lord with all our heart, believing he is able and wise to do what is best for us. In all our ways that prove pleasant, in which we gain our point of trust, and acknowledge God with thankfulness. Remember that God knows your heart. Either you will trust Him or trust in the wisdom of men, because God will not go against your will. The benefits in trusting God are far better than man wisdom. Man's wisdom is like the blind leading the blind; but, trusting God brings insight and victory. Requiring great efforts and strong standards to trust God gives you the ability to withstand stress. Now that you have God on the scene, failure is not an option. Remember the trapeze artist. They trust one another to perform their routine and that takes practice. Christians as well have to practice trusting God, because it is a lifestyle that progresses daily to develop that trust. The more you are developing trust in God the stronger you will become. The worldly system is an enemy to the Christian, but trusting God builds confidence and faith to overcome these worldly cares. Fight the good fight of faith and victory is triumph. (" say, I am a winner, amen").

10. Never go Back.

Renewal of the mind, seeking the kingdom of God, trusting in God, and having faith in God are the attributes that bring successful living and victory. But the most important one and most misunderstood is never going back to the worldly way of thinking and living. Your natural man is a lifestyle of sense realm knowledge. In other words you are governed by the senses. When challenges come and you are not deeply rooted in the Word of God, this could easily lead you down the road that leads to destruction. You must have purpose in your heart that the Word of God is the final authority and nothing will divert you to other wisdoms. If a dog bites you once; you don't go back and have the dog bite you again. You have to treat the worldly system the same way, never go back. Meaning when the worldly systems causes you to hit rock bottom in life, and Jesus delivered you from the systems. You don't go back into the worldly systems and hit rock bottom again .Why? Jesus came so that we are to enjoy life abundantly, to the full, till it overflows. (John10:10 amplified). Never go back into the worldly system operations because doubt and unstableness will come. You will begin to focus on your circumstances instead of God's promises. Going back into the world is like an insult to God, especially when God delivered you from the worldly systems. It going to take the power of God and effort on your part to stand strong on God's promises to separate and never go back to the world. When challenges arrives, it is easy to go back to your comfort zone, because that's where you find refuge from not dealing with the challenge. Using drugs, drinking alcohol, ignoring the problem, and laziness are some of the comfort zones that we go back to. God is our refuge and strong tower (Proverbs 18:10) which means He protects us, no matter what we are going through and confronted with.

Another reason, to never go back is so that you will not hinder the blessings God has in store for you. The blessing is the empowerment to succeed. When you decide to go back to the worldly system way of thinking, you reduce yourself to failure. We are to be strong in the Lord and in the power of His might(Ephesians 6:10) and when the cares of this world try to take you out, God is there to pull you through. That what it means to be strong in the Lord. Depending and trusting God totally brings the confidence that the worldly system is disposable and has no effect on your Christian lifestyle.

Conclusion: Standing with God.

So let's put this all in perspective. We know that the worldly system is an enemy for Christians, because worldly systems base their way of thinking according to men wisdoms that are contrary to God. Selfishness rules in this system to glorify the accomplishments that are made without spiritual revelation of God. To defeat this enemy, we have to allow the Word of God to become deep rooted in our hearts. The mind is being renewed by the Word from worldly systems to Godly interventions and spiritual wisdoms that will lead to godly character. We are to have a mind like Christ (Philippians 2:5) which will bring our thoughts in submission to God by the Holy Spirit. This mind renewal process is daily and must be consistent without doubt. Trusting God gives that confidence that there is no other way to overcome what the world has to offer to the believer. Trust God and His word is the final authority, and as believers we must be convinced of His trust. The backbone against the menace of the worldly systems is having faith in God. Faith is what keeps our hope alive (Hebrews 11:1). Complete trust, loyalty to God, and hearing God's words produce and develop faith. Believing and corresponding actions gives the believer that cutting edge for victory and success over this system. We walk by faith, not by sight (1 Corinthians 5:7) is our advantage over sensory mechanisms. Remember, Satan is going to try everything in his power to get from faith to sensory mechanism; but, we have authority over Satan and we are to use that authority (See Luke10:19).

By seeking the kingdom of God, you are making a decision to go with God's standards no matter how you feel or think. The kingdom of God is our strong tower(Psalms 61:3) and we are safe. We are convinced that victory comes with seeking and abiding with God.

Finally, never go back into the worldly systems once you have been delivered. As mentioned earlier, it is an insult to God when depending on the wisdom of men instead of God. Focus on the things of God, be obedient, and don't allow Satan to bombard your thoughts negatively. This enemy(worldly systems)will not have control over you. Renew, trust, seek, have faith, and never go back. These are the foundation of your success.

Section III
Satan-Adversary

1. Satan the Accuser.

Satan is the ultimate enemy and he is in control of the other two enemies. He controls self and he controls the worldly systems. His plan is to get you out of the will of God so that he can accuse you before God.(Revelation 12:10). Webster's definition for Satan: the rebellious angel who in Christian belief is the adversary of God and lord of evil. Satan is so cunning that he will attack your mind with ideals, thoughts, suggestions that can be so convincing, and lure you in for the bait. You bite and or take the bait Satan got you hooked. When you are hooked, Satan's influences are in control of your life. Can you remember something you did that was wrong and you knew it was wrong; but you did it any way? You were influenced by Satan. Any weakness in your Christian walk is an avenue for Satan to launch attack against your character. Satan knows he is a defeated foe and he doesn't want to be alone. Satan will always accuse believers when they fall away from the truth because Satan needs bodies to carry out his assignment or plan.

What is Satan's plan? Destruction, confusion, deception, fear, and any motives that are contrary to God's will. As a deceiver, he is great at making people believe he doesn't exist. This is Satan at his best because if you don't believe he is real; he will have his way with you without detection. This is one of Satan's deceptions; to operate without being detected. Now, once you become born-again the spirit will reveal who Satan is. The light shines on his darkness and Satan can't hide any longer from the body of Christ. Satan is an enemy to our soul. He is subtle and delights in deception. He is shrewd in his operations, cunning, and crafty.

Satan is the enemy of the righteous and of those who seek to do the will of God. Satan is also a tempter of mankind. Satan will keep people in bondage for his glory. Satan's purpose is to keep you confused and not trusting God, living out your own way by depending on man's wisdom instead of God. Christians have to be aware of Satan's devices (2Corinthians 2:11) and put him where he belongs.

2. The Origin of Satan(Devil)

Satan was once an angel, known as Lucifer, the son of the morning star.(Isaiah 14:12). Something happened to Lucifer, because he wanted to be like or above God. So Satan devised a plan against God. Satan was so convincing that he would be above God that some of the angels moved to his side. Then, there was a war in Heaven (Revelation 12:7-9), Satan and his angels lost and was cast out of Heaven to the Earth. This is why Satan is known to be the god of this world (2 Corinthians 4:4). Satan wants to steal, kill, and destroy Christians.(John10:10a). Mobilizing his cohorts(demons) to deploy his strategies against the kingdom of God. What makes Satan so effective that he will reason with you and twist the truth in a way that you begin to rationalize with man's wisdom, instead of Godly truth. This was the way he got to Eve in the garden, causing her to reason with what God told her not to do. (Read Genesis 3 the Fall of Man).

Now back to the origin of Satan. Pride was Satan's downfall in Heaven because he wanted to be like God. (Isaiah 14:12-15). Satan led the revolt in Heaven; his angels against God's angels and he lost. He was cast out of Heaven; along with his angels (known as fallen angels) into the Earth(Revelation 12:9). For the god of this world has blinded the unbelievers minds:[that they should not discern the truth], preventing them from seeing the illuminating light of the gospel of the glory of Christ(the

Messiah), who is the image and the likeness of God.(2 Corinthians 4:4 amplified bible). Satan is manipulating this world for the assassination of Christians and mankind together. He causes havoc, loss, devastation, and ruin and that is the norm of his behavior. There's nothing good in Satan's personality and there will never be any good. Nowhere in the Bible do you see Satan doing anything good. He rebellious against God and Satan is making sure that he is not the only one that is rebellious against the kingdom of God. Just like the fallen angels that sided with him in Heaven, there's a generation of people who worship him like a god, and this generation feels that this is the right way to live. Today, internet, occults, and spirit of darkness sect indulge in such practices. As believers we must fight to get our young generation back to the truth and serving God.

3. Bait of Satan.

Fishermen use bait to catch fish, something that will attract the fish to the hook. What is bait? Bait can be a ambush, decoy, lure, snare, attraction, enticement,seduction, and temptation. Satan uses bait to lure believers into disobedience before God. For instance, you were an alcoholic and you gave your life to Christ. You got cleaned up and sober. One day an old friend you had not seen for a long time shows up at the door with your favorite bottle(label) of booze. Satan knows it your favorite label, so you have a choice. Take the bait which is the booze and fail or let your friend know that you're sober and don't drink any more. That's how Satan operates; to bait or entice you to give in. Once you take the bait, then that puts Satan in control over the situation. Satan focuses on your weakness, he knows when, where, and how to bring that weakness to focus. Satan will lure you to your past shortcomings to make you feel condemned; to get you thinking that God doesn't care. Remember, Satan will use thoughts, ideals, and suggestions to bait you. We can't allow Satan to take advantage. We as Christians are not ignorant of his devices. (2 Corinthians 2:11). No matter what bait Satan tries to use, we are not to be lured in. When you are strong in the Lord and the power of his might (Ephesians 6:10), then the bait of Satan has no effect.

Another way Satan will bait you is by transforming into an angel of light.(2 Corinthians 11:14). Satan is a great imitator of the truth. Satan can twist the truth in a way to make it so convincing even though it's a lie. The twist will be something that is contrary to the word of God. The Holy Spirit will help us to discern these ungodly truths, so that we will not be confused to the real truth. The truth, which is the Word of God, is an enemy to Satan because it will bring destruction to any of Satan's assignment to the believer. Also the word will set the captive free. When sinners give their life to Christ, Satan immediately show up on the scene to snatch the word from the believer's heart. (Matthew 13:19). The reason why Satan shows up is because the believer is now equipped with authority to fight, and another one he loses from the kingdom of darkness.

Satan is not alone in this spiritual warfare. Fallen angels and demons are in this battle also and Satan is the leader. Giving orders to his cohorts on what assignments to carry out. That's why the Bible says that we wrestle not against flesh and blood, but against principalities, powers, ruler of darkness, and spiritual wickedness(Ephesians 6:12). The media or movies make Satan a powerful force. In movies where he defeats the priest, there is no power in the cross or blood, all fiction. In reality, Satan wants you to think that he his power, but he doesn't.

Satan is the constant enemy to God, to Christ, to the divine kingdom, to the followers of Christ, and to all truth; full of falsehood, malice, and seducing people to evil in every possible way. The popular notion is that Satan is the enemy of man and active in misleading and cursing humanity because of his intense opposition to God.

4. Works of Satan.

The worldwide and age long works of Satan, are to be traced to one predominate motive. Satan hates both God and mankind and does all he can to defeat God's plan of grace and to establish and maintain a kingdom of evil in the seduction and ruin of mankind. Satan has no respect of person and is working hard on bringing havoc to the kingdom of God. Remember, he was an angelic being known as Lucifer, pride was his demise which caused him to be kicked out of Heaven. Now Satan is at war. Satan will keep you in bondage, confused, lacking faith and confidence in the promises of God. Satan wants you back to your comfort zone or backsliding into the kingdom of darkness. Backslide means to revert back to your worldly or natural man way of thinking and living. You stop going to church, stop praying, stop giving offers, and stop trusting God. This is how Satan operates, to stop the anointing that God has place on your life. Satan hates Christians and will stop at nothing to cause Christians to fail. If Satan can get in your mind and screw with your thinking, he will screw with your actions. Hosea 4:6 states,"my people are destroyed by the lack of knowledge." Satan will bombard your thoughts and if you don't have knowledge of the thing, will make you a victim instead of a victor.

Let's look at some other alias for Satan.

1. the dragon-Revelation 12:9
2. the old serpent-Revelation 20:2
3. the prince of this world-John 12:31&14:30
4. the prince of the power of the air-Ephesians 2:2
5. the god of this world-2 Corinthians 4:4
6. a roaring lion-1 Peter 5:8
7. the devil-Hebrews 2:14 & Matthew 4:1
8. accuser of our brethren-Revelation 12:10
9. adversary-1Peter 5:8
10. angel of the bottomless pit-Revelation 9:11
11. enemy-Matthew 13:39
12. evil spirit-1Samuel 16:14
13. father of lies-John 8:44
14. power of darkness-Colossians 1:13
15. tempter-Matthew 4:3 & 1Thessalonians 3:5
16. unclean spirit-Matthew 12:43
17. wicked one-Matthew 13:19

Satan disguises himself to complete the assignments that he set up against the kingdom of God. As Christians we need to be aware, so that we can stand up to his deception. Satan will not play fair, his motives are to present havoc to your character, and accuse you before the throne of God. That why it is important to use the Word of God as a weapon to defeat Satan plans and the cohorts that carry out his plans. Remember Satan knows the Word of God too, but he will twist the truth to make the word so convincing for his glory. You have to know who you are in Christ to veto the cunningness of Satan and not deviate from the truth.

5. "The Devil made me Do It"

Have you heard this old adage, "the devil made me do it," when stepping into sin or doing something wrong? Well it's a true statement sometimes, but not all the time. What I'm going to focus on here is the influences Satan has on individuals. There are times when situations in life occur and we can't blame God or Satan, because we can make foolish mistakes. The motive of Satan(devil) is to over shadow you with doubt and disbelief about the things of God. Trust God to always have the solution to the situations. There's a war between the flesh and the spirit and Satan operates within the flesh. Walk in the spirit and you shall not fulfill the lust of the flesh.(Galatians 5:16-17). Lust is an intense craving that will draw you away from the truth. Satan is such a great deceiver, that what you lust for he will bring to your remembrance. If you are not careful you will fall into his trap. Paul defined the Christian struggle in (See Romans7:15-21) and Paul was clear about the daily war internal and Satan is a part of this reason that we fight internally. Satan will start with the weakest link and use deception. Satan will bind your mind, causing confusion to defeat you and your ability to claim victory. Satan is so crafty that he makes you believe the thoughts are your own. The thoughts of a stranger you will not know, but your thoughts are noticeable. Let me give an example, when Jesus was tempted in the wilderness (Luke 4), Satan didn't just walk up to Jesus one on one asking questions. If he had Jesus would have immediately known who Satan was, right? Therefore Satan used another approach, He attacked Jesus through the mind. If Satan can get you to reason with the truth, then Satan will deceive by twisting the truth. Jesus knew who Satan was and took authority over him with the Word of God(as it is written). "So the devil made me do it," huh. How? Through your thought life. It is very important to guard your thoughts, because that is Satan's territory. Satan will steal, kill, and destroy you. That's his motive (John10:10a). He has no way of getting to you, except through the mind. Satan will come to you with thoughts, ideas,and suggestions that will oppose the things of God. It's a spiritual battle that we must win. Satan wants you out of control concerning your thought life and having an unstable mind is Satan's objective. Depression, fear, and unbelief means that the Christian had a battle on the situation and lost. Therefore don't dwell on the wiles of the devil, the evil day, and fiery darts, but claim victory with the armor God gives you on the battlefield.(Ephesians 6:13-17).

6. An Angel of Light.

Paul in his writing to the Corinthians warned them of satanic transformation. "For such are false apostles, deceitful workers, transforming themselves into apostles of Christ. And no wonder! For Satan himself transforms himself into an angel of light.(2Corinthians 11:13-14). Satan is very good in using a willing vessel (person) to distort the truth. There are angels from heaven preaching other gospels that are not of God.(Galatians1:8-10). This is why there are so many different denominations of religion; because of an angel preaching a gospel with twisted truth. Satan is very persuasive in this arena because Satan knows that there's only one way to Heaven, and he will make you think there are other ways to the Father. Jesus made it quiet clear that there is only one way to the Father.(John14:6).

Satan assignment is to keep as many people from the true nature of God way of living and thinking, and his cohorts are with him to carry out these assignments. Hell was only for Satan and his fallen angels; not for people. But the plan of Satan was, "if I go down then others are going down with me". Therefore, be careful who you come in contact with, for they could be that angel of light. They could be so convincing that you begin to seek their wisdom instead of God's. That why discernment of spirits is so important for the believers. The Holy Spirit will not lead you astray, but down the path of truth. Satan is not ignorant of the truth but will twist the truth in another way that will and could lead you astray. Could it be possible to succumb to Satan's trickery. Yes. How? When you are not deep rooted or mature in the things of God, Satan will come along and seduce and attack the mind with thoughts, ideals, and suggestions that are going to be contrary to the truth. But it will appear so convincing that you will lose focus on the one that saved you. Satan operates in darkness, deception, and lies which make up his character. Pride was his downfall in Heaven. Since he lost that battle in Heaven, Satan became an instant enemy to God, and now his plan is to cause havoc to the body of Christ. Darkness is the opposite of lightness and Satan domain is darkness. This darkness isn't the natural kind of darkness(night). This type of darkness is deception of the truth. I like to think of it this way darkness-deception and lightness-truth and Satan uses both. Yes he knows the Bible, but he will twist the truth for his advantage. That's why he is called an angel of light; but, behind this disguise darkness is there. The truth is not in Satan and there will always be damage intervention to the body of Christ, until he is cast into the lakes of fire(hell) (Revelation 20:10). We have to be alert and diligently seeking God for guidance into the affairs of Satan. This is only the tip of the iceberg on how Satan operates. but giving you insight of this enemy can give us an advantage. Now let's discuss ways of having victory over this menace.

7. The New Creation.

Satan is the father of sinners and God is the father of believers. Therefore we must transfer from a sinner into the family of God. The way to become a Christian is to be born-again. Being born-again is the first step in defeating Satan. How to be born-again? Jesus came into this world to destroy the works of the devil (John3:8) and to save mankind. Being born-again is an act of faith to allow Jesus to be your savior and deliver you from darkness (Satan territory) to the marvelous light. You come to Jesus a sinner and confess with your mouth the lord Jesus to come in your heart and Jesus will save you. "That if you confess with your mouth the lord Jesus and believe in your heart that God has raised Him from the dead, you will be saved".(Romans 10:9nkjv)

Once that confession is made, you are a new creature in Christ. Old things are passed away and new things become new. (2 Corinthians 5:17). The spirit(inner man) becomes alive and you will begin your journey as a Christian which is a process and progression into the newness of life. This journey will be a battle, but you have authority that God has given you for success in this journey. (see Luke 10:19). When you accept Jesus as your Lord and personal savior, Satan shows up immediately to put doubt in your mind about your salvation.("are you sure that you are saved, look you still doing the same thing as before"). The reason why Satan shows up is because of the benefits you will have as a Christian, plus you're not under the control of Satan anymore. Using your authority in Christ will defeat any influence that Satan will send your way. For as many as are led by the spirit of God they are the sons of God. (Romans 8:14) We are sons and daughters of the living God because of the new birth. Jesus has brought you out of the family of Satan and placed you into the family of God with authority over the enemy. Life for the believer should be better than that of a sinner, because of the relationship that is established with God. There will be a prayer for salvation at the end of this book.

8. Authority the Key.

Webster's definition of authority: a power of influences or commands thought, opinion, or behavior, freedom granted by one in authority, a person in command. Synonym: power. God has given us authority over Satan and his cohorts. Let's look at authority in action. A policeman is directing traffic, he holds his hand up and blows the whistle commanding you to stop your car. You have the ability to keep going or maybe run the policeman over, but you don't. Why? You respect the authority the policeman has and if you disobey his command there will be consequences. The policeman knows he has the city government to back any decision he makes. The Christians have the same authority the policeman has, but the believer has Heaven government to back them up and Satan knows this. We are God's policeman on Earth. Christians are not to back down to Satan and his cohorts, but to use our authority against them and have victory over them. When you become born-again you have authority instantly, with the affect of starting to bind the spirit of darkness right away. There's nothing in the kingdom of darkness that can hurt you when you know who you are in Christ. "Behold, I give unto you power(authority)to tread on serpents and scorpions, and over all the power(ability) of the enemy: and nothing shall by any means hurt you.(Luke 10:19) This scripture is a powerful statement and the believer needs to meditate on this scripture to get it deep rooted in their spirit. So, when the wiles of the devil comes, the evil day, and fiery darts come we are ready to exercise the authority that God has blessed us with. Be strong in the Lord, and in the power of his might (authority).(Ephesians 6:10). We can overcome resistance and not allow Satan to penetrate our hearts and minds. Submit yourselves therefore to God. Resist the devil(Satan) and he will flee from you.(James 4:7). You want Satan to leave you alone for a season? Submit to God. It's important to submit to God because that is where your authority will come from. When you use your authority on Satan, he has no choice but to flee. (You want Satan to flee? Use your authority). We are Heaven policemen to make arrests in the kingdom of darkness upon this Earth. To arrest any evil that is contrary to God. To arrest negative ideals, thoughts, and suggestions that Satan puts on us to sin against God.

Jesus made a powerful statement after His resurrection. "And Jesus came and spake to them(disciples) saying, all authority has been given to Me in Heaven and on Earth(Matthew 28:18nkjv). What an awesome statement. This is letting the believer know that they have the same authority Jesus has. This is why it very important to use authority on situations that will bring doubt to your spirit. Authority is released by our confessions. Confession is simply saying or making a statement with your mouth. When the cares of this world invade your spirit, open your mouth and make confessions of faith to overturn your despair into strength and victory. Confession releases authority by which a stand is made not to be moved from the truth. Death and life are in the power of the tongue and those who love it will eat its fruit. (Proverbs18:21nkjv) You can speak life with authority to your situations or speak death out of fear. Your mouth is your weapon. The devil will try to shut you up. The worst thing believers can do is to shut their mouths and stop praising God.

9. Spiritual Tactics.

A military soldier has to know which military tactics to use against the enemy to defeat them. The same holds true for the believer engaged in spiritual warfare; to know which spiritual tactics to use against the enemy to claim victory. Tactics are skills used in employing available means to accomplish and end and maneuvering forces in combat. We are definitely on the battlefield with the forces of darkness and spiritual tactics are vital for a successful victory. Listed below are some spiritual tactics that can be used against the enemy.

1. The Word of God.
2. Guidance of the Holy Spirit.
3. Faith.
4. Love.

When these spiritual tactics are put to their proper use, you will win the battle.

First, the Word of God. God's will is in His Word, it is our instruction manual for all issues in life that we encounter daily. "All scriptures are given by inspiration of God and are profitable, for doctrine, for reproof, for correction, for instructions in righteousness. (2 Timothy 3:16). Let this word be deep rooted in your heart(spirit) to keep the enemy confused or brought to ruins. Let the Word of Christ dwell in you richly in all wisdom. The

Word of God is a powerful tactic to use to overtake this enemy. When Jesus was tempted in the wilderness by the devil, Jesus used the Word against him by saying "it is written." Christians are to be like Jesus when dealing with Satan, open our mouth with the Word of God to close out any demonic influences The Word has power; a force that is to be reckoned with. God's Word has the power to penetrate all pretense and discernment of thoughts and intents of the heart. Your mouth is the instrument used to speak the Word of God against Satan. We have to be careful not to allow Satan to snatch that Word from our heart's because Satan knows that the Word of God is death to his plans. Again the worst thing a believer can do is to shut up and stop praising God. The Word brings victory, the Word brings success, and the Word will put you in another dimension of your Christian stability with God. Submitting to the Word will cause Satan to flee, because you are putting up resistance to his trickery and any assignments that were given to his cohorts against you (James 4:7). Bible knowledge is vitally important, without the Word you are setting yourself up to be destroyed for the lack of knowledge (Hosea 4:6). The thief comes to steal, kill, and destroy (John 10:10a). When your ammunition is the Word of God, you will reverse what Satan intends to do. For instance, taking back the dreams that were stolen from you. Take the Word and kill any thoughts by casting them down, plus destroy any fiery darts. This is how the Word will work if used properly.

Remember the Word of God is your best defense against Satan. Also, the Word is communication of God's will to mankind. All knowledge is obtained from the Word of God. The Word has authority, which is needed for the battle.

Keep the Word richly in your heart and you will overcome any obstacles that Satan will put in your pathway.

The guidance of the Holy Spirit is another spiritual tactic that is used against Satan warfare. As believers we must yield to the Holy Spirit. Jesus made it clear to his disciples that it was imperative for Him to leave so that the Comforter would come. "The Comforter which is the Holy Ghost whom the Father will send in my name (Jesus), he shall teach you all things, and bring all things to your remembrance, whatsoever I have said unto you".(John 14:26). The Holy Spirit is all truth, which is the truth of God, and is still carrying out the mission of God today. The Holy Spirit(Holy Ghost) is the third person of the Trinity(God-Son-Holy Spirit). The Holy Spirit reproves, helps, glorifies, and intercedes.(John 16:7-13 & Romans 8:26). He is omnipresent(Psalms 139:7 & Ephesians 2:17-13), omniscient(1 Corinthians 2:10-11), and omnipotent (Luke 1:35 & Romans 8:11). The Holy Spirit carries power, a conviction of the truth into the heart of mankind. The Holy Spirit will guide you to the truth and will help bring the Word to battle against the forces of darkness. We understand where our powers come from: "But ye shall receive power, after that the Holy Ghost is come upon you (Acts1:8). Our directions comes from the Holy Spirit. "For as many are led by the Spirit of God they are the sons of God." (Romans 8:14)

The guidance of the Holy Spirit should be used as a spiritual tactic against Satan, because the Holy Spirit is there for us in times of weakness and for prayer. "Likewise the Spirit also helps our infirmities: for we know not what we should pray for as we ought: but the Spirit itself makes intercession for us with groaning which cannot be uttered."

(Romans 8:26). Soldiers have a rifle for protection at war. The Holy Spirit is a rifle for the believers in spiritual battles. "For we do not wrestle against flesh and blood, but against principalities, against powers, against the rulers of the darkness of this age, and against spiritual host of wickedness in the heavenly places (Ephesians 6:12nkjv). The Holy Spirit is our defense to overcome any devices that Satan tries to put on Christians. We are to triumph in everything we face and the Holy Spirit will make victory a reality. We are winners and in all these things we are more than conquerors through Him who loves us (Romans 8:37nkjv). Remember the Holy Spirit guides the believer in all truth with what he hears from the Father and the Son(John 15:26). The tactic that Satan fears the most is when the truth is revealed to the Christian. "Howbeit when he, the Spirit of truth is come, he will guide you into all truth(John 16:13a). "And you shall know the truth, and the truth shall make you free."(John 8:32). Once you are free from Satan's lies, you are no longer controlled by Satan. Freedom is far better than being in bondage. Freedom produces peace and bondage produces fear. The Holy Spirit cares about our well being and has given us authority to carry out the plans of God for a successful living.

Another tactic used against Satan is Faith. Faith is acting on the Word of God. Faith in Christ secures for the believer freedom from condemnation and the circumstances that surround them. Faith is what we hold on to until what we are believing for is manifest. Faith is essentially an act of trusting God. Faith is a part of the Christian's life from the beginning to the end. "Now faith is the substance of things hoped for, the evidence of things not seen (Hebrews 11:1). That's why it's important to trust

God for the things not seen. Jesus appeared to his disciples after his resurrection and Thomas wasn't there. Thomas made a statement, "I will not believe unless I see the marks of his hands and touch his side". Jesus appeared to Thomas and showed the marks on his hands and side. Then Jesus said to Thomas, "bless are those who have not seen, but yet believe (John 20:24-29). Which faith do you have?-the God kind of faith?-or Thomas faith? Satan knows of this kind of faith and in his power keep you in the Thomas kind of faith. Faith in action will keep you on course to reach the destiny God planned for your life. Faith is our backbone, trust, confidence, reliable, and charges us to push forward in hard times. God provides the substance for all things we hope for through His word. Faith is not some kind of movement, but a law. The scripture tell the believer to "walk by faith, not by sight (2 Corinthians 5:7). Everything in the kingdom of God operates by faith. Confidence is faith which brings assurance that God will work out the situation by being obedient to the things of God. Form a habit of living and walking by faith on a daily basis, because Satan can't stand to be around positive thinking believers when faith is in action. We have to step beyond natural circumstances of life, and step in the supernatural flow of God, and faith will make this possible. The shield of faith quenches Satan's fiery darts(Ephesians 6:16). The shield is protection, but action has to be applied to the shield to be affective. In other words, a soldier who doesn't hold up his shield in battle is prone to be injured or killed, but when he holds up the shield then there is protection, because of the action he took. Faith is the same way, corresponding actions applied will produce protection and victory.

Without faith it is impossible to please God(Hebrews 11:6a). Without the God kind of faith you are putting your faith in man wisdom. The wisdom of man is temporal vs God faith which is everlasting. A choice has to be made when you are against the wall and it seems there is no way out, will it be man wisdom or the God's kind of faith. The spiritual tactic of faith will always defeat Satan. Remember, Satan will counter attack by making you think that faith isn't real or that faith will not work. When you are strong and know who you are in Christ, it doesn't matter what Satan thinks, because the truth is revealed and freedom is yours for the taking. To live a victorious life style faith can't be dormant, it must be developed, exercised, and become strong. The sky is the limit and beyond for believers when faith is put in action. Have faith in God.(Mk11:22)

The spiritual tactic of love, Satan's worst nightmare. (Read 1 Corinthians 13). The greatest commandment that Jesus gave was "Thou shalt love the Lord thy God with all thy heart, and with all thy soul, and with all thy mind. This is the first and great commandment. And the second is like unto it. Thou shalt love thy neighbor as thyself". (Matthew 22:37-39) A new commandment I give unto you, that ye also love one another (John13:34). Notice how Jesus added great and new to the love commandments, the greatest attribute a person can have is love and a new attitude and heart to express this love. This kind of love that is expressed in the Bible is unconditional love and it not based on selfish gain. God is love(1John 4:8, 16) just as truly as He is "light"(1 John 1:5) "truth"(1John 1:6) and "spirit"(John 4:24). For God so loved the world, that he gave his only begotten Son(John 3:16a). This was the way God showed his love to mankind. Therefore we must express our love in the same manner. "We love, because he first loved us"(1John 4:19). God not only loved the world and mankind, but this love was special and genuine.

Since God loved us, we have to make sure that mankind is loved also. There is nothing that can separate this kind of love when sowed in your heart. Love is taking the initiative to build up and meet the needs of others without expecting anything in return. Love desires to seek and apply what God's words have to say. God's love must be our model for a life time. Love must flow into us from Christ and in return flow out from us to those around us. God's love is the ultimate power for Christians to use as a spiritual tactic against Satan's hatred. We are to be fueled and empowered to love at all times and in any given situation. Love is the turning of our backs to self concerns and facing our neighbor's concerns. That's why Satan hates this spiritual tactic of love, we are focused on the other person's needs to bring them into a place of comfort and love. Jesus was the perfect example of how love is to be express. When Jesus showed up on the scene, multitude of people followed, Jesus didn't go to the people. The people came to Him. Why? The love Jesus had in his heart attracted people to him. We have to let unconditional love saturate our hearts in a way that attract people to us. Love has no boundaries, no restrictions, not selfish. Love produces meekness, an attitude of humility towards God and gentleness towards mankind.

We have to let love work in us and through us to be fully successful in our Christian walk. People are watching you and waiting for you to make a mistake to criticize you, but when love is shining so bright in your heart, the critics will begin to want what you have, which is love. Jesus loved us as a friend. We need to love others in this fashion and want to see the one we loved to grow to their full potential. There is no jealousy in love, God's love in us prompts us to give of ourselves. The world will identify a Christian by the love they share and when love is shared the world senses harmony and peace. Love is a very strong and successful spiritual tactic against Satan. Satan will use everything in his arsenal to destroy this kind of love. Unconditional love can't be penetrated by Satan when you are strong and mature in Christ. When you show love to your enemies, especially the ones that are close to you Satan goes ballistic. Why would you want to show love? Because in the natural you want to get even, But Jesus taught us the opposite and that was to love one another. Love that is exercised pleases the Lord and puts your enemy at peace with you(Proverbs 16:7). Here's an example. Let's say a person you work with becomes upset with you. Maybe it was something you said that caused that person to get ticked off. The person who is upset is waiting for a response in an argumentative way. On the other hand , your response is soft and loving and even apologetic. This type of response confuses the other person, because it wasn't what they expected. Showing love brings peace to the matter at hand. God want us to be problem solvers with love instead of consumed with the-eye-for-an-eye syndrome. God is love

Conclusion.

The number one enemy the believer face is Satan and his cohorts. Satan's master plan is to steal, kill, destroy Christians. He controls the act of selfishness, "Big Mr. I," and the operations of the worldly systems known as the world. Satan is deceptive, cunning, and makes his lies seem so truthful. Satan is undetected to some because they don't believe he exists or is real; which is Satan's greatest deception. To the believer, Satan is the enemy that must be dealt with. Satan only has three weapons ideals, thoughts, and suggestions. The vulnerable area Satan attack is the mind. He will also use the eye gate, ear gate, and the mouth gate. That's why it is so important to guard your mind. Keep the mind free from distractions so that the Holy Spirit can flow freely. Satan is the accuser of the brethren(Revelation 12:10) and is looking for ways to point out your shortcomings or sins to God. Don't be fooled by Satan's cunningness, because he knows that time is limited and wants the believer to fail, and go down the path of destruction for his glory. Hell is intended for Satan and his cohorts, but Satan is on a mission to bring other with him. He is sparing no expense to carry out this mission to its fullness. Therefore, we can't give no place to the devil(Ephesians 4:27), because Satan wants to control your way of living. Let the truth be known, Satan is out to get you. Thanks be to God, we have authority over this defeated foe. We have the word of God to saturate our spirits and renew our minds for strength. That which is spiritually true can be used to our advantage against Satan's deceitfulness. We have the authority that God has given the believer to use against Satan to claim victory. Authority that is not used will give Satan an open avenue for deception. Christians are well equipped to stand against the spirit of darkness. God is light in Him there is no darkness(1 John 1:5). When light shines; darkness disappears. A thief loves to operate in darkness because he does not want to be detected or seen. This is Satan's modus operandi(MO), but where there is light then he is detected on the wrong that he wants to afflict on you. Light foils any plans of Satan and the word of God that is confessed out of your mouth will defeat Satan and victory is ours for the taking.

Spiritual tactics when used properly win battles. These tactics are to be developed and become permanent in your Christian walk and arsenal. The Bible speaks of the armor of God(see Ephesians 6:10-18). You are a soldier for Christ and spiritual tactics are plans used against the enemy. Spiritual warfare is constantly going on around us daily and we must be ready to defend ourselves. Being alert and using our authority, because the adversary will not rest until he sees a weakness in your line of defense. When you know who you are in Christ, being strong, have power, and having on the armor of God, Satan will be unable to find any weakness and Satan will flee for a season. Stay in Christ, study the Word, prayer, and just be committed to the things of God. When Satan returns and he will return, he will find you mature and stable, which means that Satan will keep moving on. Spiritual tactics are to be embraced at all times and deployed when negative circumstances arise.

The truth of the matter is that our battle on the battlefield is not with flesh and blood. Being alerted to what we are up against has it advantages. Weakness with this battle causes fear and will allow Satan to penetrate the line of defense against him. Once that line of defense is broken, then Satan has control which will led to destruction. " The Lord is my light and my salvation: whom shall I fear? The Lord is the strength of life: of whom shall I be afraid. (Psalms 27:1). "We may boldly say, The Lord is my helper, and I will not fear what man shall do unto me.(Hebrews 13:6). As you can see, fear is not an option when it comes to spiritual battle. Strength and love cast out fear and when you are strong fear disappears (1John 4:18). "For God hath not given us the spirit of fear, but of power, and of love, and of a sound mind.(1 Timothy 1:7).

Satan is our enemy, he will not slumber to get you out of the will of God. Just like God is no respecter of person, so is Satan no respecter of person. Victory over Satan is achieved when you know who you are in Christ. We have ammunition to kill any plans that Satan sets before us. Let's keep this enemy under our feet where he belongs by meeting any challenges with the correct spiritual tactics. Don't let Satan rule, but let Christ rule and live a life that is victorious and prosperous. God rewards you for your diligence by seeking first His kingdom(Matthew 6:33).

After Thoughts

This book is designed to expose the enemy's ways of operations and how to make plans and strategies against these enemies. The three most common enemies are: 1."The Big Mr. I" which is selfishness; 2. the world known as the worldly systems, which is base on men wisdom and philosophies; and 3.Satan our adversary, the accuser of the brethren to God. Our spiritual warfare is up against these three enemies on a daily basis. These enemies are unavoidable, but can be contained easily with the authority we have for victory. The words that come out of our mouths will determine our success over these enemies. You can speak life or death into situations. (Proverbs 18:21). Our spiritual defenses and tactics have authority that will defeat these enemies easily. Our body is the temple of God, and that the Spirit of God dwelling in you 1 Corinthians 3:16), which will keep the enemy at bay, for you have been set aside to serve God. Since the body is the temple for the Spirit, that gives us the authority and strength over the spirit of darkness. Boundaries are set by the Holy Spirit for the believer and the truth is in our heart and that which is not true is kept away. So our advantage is the temple of God and the temple must be kept clean. The devil will boggle your mind with all sorts of negative and selfish needs; to the point that you begin to apply human reasonings or wisdom on setting the situation at hand instead of seeking God's answer. That's how cunning Satan is, to divert your spiritual thinking. Alertness of Satan's devices has it advantages. Looking to any plan that's going to cause you to fall from the will of God. We overcome these devices by exercising the authority that God has blessed us with and put that enemy under our feet where he belongs (1Corinthians 15:25).

When the enemy is exposed, remember the enemy likes to operate in darkness, you know which spiritual tactic to counter for resistance. Just as we know about the enemy, the enemy knows about us. Satan wants to interrupt your well being to cause you to doubt, and not trusting God. He wants to make you believe that the promises of God will not work for you. Satan's master plan is for you to give up and journey back to the way of living before you were born-again. The "Big Mr. I", the worldly systems, and our adversary Satan are the spirit of darkness' tactics against Christians, and if not careful or aware of them, could lead you to spiritual separation and spiritual death. The thief comes to kill, steal, and destroy: Jesus came so we can have life in abundance, to the full, and till it overflows (John 10:10 amplified bible). Choose life and defeat the enemy. Trials and tribulations are a part of the Christians life, but we are to hold our peace and have good cheer (John 16:33). Trisls and tribulation are tests to see who you will trust, God's wisdom or Satan's wisdom. When you know who you are in Christ it is a no-brainer on who you will choose, because you have the authority of heaven to back you up.

These enemies are not in the market of being fair. Selfishness, keeping you from the truth, bitterness, and unforgivingness are just a few things that bring havoc to a Christian. We deal with opposition daily and we need a line of defense at all times to avoid becoming a victim. Opposition to the truth brings confusion to the body of Christ. We need to be on guard; prepare to attack the enemy head on.

This book is for the believer to have advantages over the enemy and claim victory for a successful life Having confidence, knowledge, and resistance is the key to overthrowing the enemy. Lack of knowledge and the enemy will destroy you(Hosea 4:6). The battlefield will require knowledge of the Word of God as ammunition against the spirit of darkness. Spending time in the Word is very important because the enemy will attack at any time. Readiness is the key. Confessing the Word daily builds confidence in our spirit(inner man); which results in victory. Can victory be achieved by doubt, No! Can victory be achieved when sin is present? No way! Victory can be achieved by focusing on seeking the kingdom of God first and it's righteousness(Matthew 6:33). Making the Word of God the final authority will bring stability. Satan will keep you from the Word as much as possible because of the power the Word has over him and his cohorts. When light shines on darkness, (light being the Word), darkness is exposed to the truth, and Satan's deception is rendered useless. That's how we want Satan-useless and powerless. Unity within the Body of Christ makes these enemies unable to penetrate our character in Christ.

Lets keep in mind that there will be spiritual warfare at all times. What we learn about spiritual tactics assure us that victory is a part of living a prosperous life. Christians are to be strong and not cave in or give up when circumstances get tough; but, use the weapons God blessed us with. You will see a major difference in your Christian walk when the authority you have over the kingdom of darkness is used. "Behold, I give you power(authority) to tread on serpents and scorpions, and over all the power(ability) of the enemy: and nothing shall by and means hurt you"(Luke 10:19). "Submit therefore to God: Resist the devil, and he will flee from you."(James 4:7). You want victory in your life? Use the authority, resistance, faithfulness, and love of God in your spirit. Then the devil will flee for a season and fruit will come when you hold fast to your confession. "He shall be like a tree planted by the rivers of water, that bring forth its fruit in its season, whose leaf also shall not wither: and whatever he does shall prosper".(Psalms 1:3njkv).

After Thoughts Part Two

The "Big Mr. I"-selfishness.
World–Worldly Systems.
Satan-Adversary.

Are any of these three enemies governing your life? How can you tell? Seeking ways to gain fame and attention by manipulation of others for your glory without regard for others, that will put you in that category of selfishness. Are you selfish? Maybe you are a news or media buff, constantly watching to see what this world is offering; which is not a whole lot. Stock market woes, bank failure, unemployment, and health care issues, and you're watching to see when the turn around is going come. Therefore you are trusting in man wisdom and ideals to pull you through this recession. The worldly systems are designed to keep you down and guessing on life's challenges, and we become stressed out because of these challenges. Is this you? Lastly, Satan is our adversary; the accuser of the brethren. Deception, unforgivingness, and hatred is his personality. His ultimate plan is to take you from the will of God. Satan's greatest deception is making you believe that he is not real. When you fall for that bait then Satan is in control of your life. Jesus came to destroy the works of the devil(1 John 3:8). Has Satan conquered you? Let's not succumbed to these enemies because they will disrupt your maturity in the things of God.

The battlefield of darkness will bring challenges for the believer and alertness is necessary to meet these challenges for victory. Life for the believer is to be far better than the life of a sinner. As Christians, you must be deeply rooted in God's Word. That how you build confidence; which is faith that can face any challenges and win. We can't be victims to these enemies, we are to stand on what we believe in Christ Jesus. Jesus has won this battle for us (John 16:33). He is our champion and we are to follow the example that he left us with. (John 13:15). Don't be discouraged when it appears nothing is working or not being manifested, this is one of Satan's deceptions, remember the Holy Spirit will lead you to all truth and that what you believe in will come to past. Patience is a virtue for the believer, along with faith and the battle is won.

Let this book be your guide to put together strategies that will produce a line of defense against these enemies. Victorious living is what Christians strive for to represent God's best in their lives, which is an affective witness to others. Once a person sees how successful you are they will be attracted to you. "Let your light so shine before men, that they may see your works, and glorify your Father which is in Heaven."(Matthew 5:16). We give our best because God gave His best-Jesus Christ his only begotten son.

We live in a society that allows the abnormal to be normal. Things like same sex marriages, abortions, fornication, and homosexuality, naming only a few, and Satan is front runner of these practices. That's why we are God's policemen on this Earth to arrest anything that is out of the will of God. God's words are true and will never change, Christians need this Word in their hearts to be strong, mature, and resist any snares that these enemies have set before you. "Let not your heart be troubled..."(John 14:1a). We have weapons. Faith, love, authority, and confessions of God's word will destroy the enemy. How do you want your life to be? Full of stress, confusion, and failure or victory, prosperity, and peace. God made man in his image and gave him dominion and authority. He also gave man a will to choose a quality life. "I call heaven and earth as witnesses today against you , that I set before you life and death, blessing and cursing: therefore choose life, that both you and your descendants may live."(Deuteronomy 30:19). As Christians we are going to have to learn how to apply Biblical knowledge to our lives, if we want to win the battles of life. We can have victory in life by being strong in the Lord and in the power of His might.(Ephesians 6:10) Is there anything too hard for God? I don't think so. Satan wants you to think it hard and there is no way out; but, our God is there for the rescue. "With men this is impossible, but with God all things are possible."(Matthew 19:26).

    Let's look at how we can overcome these enemies 1.Big Mr. I-Selfishness vs. showing love and taking care of the needs of others.2. World-Worldly Systems vs. seek the kingdom of God first.3.Satan-Adversary vs. Submit to God and resist. There are many ways to overcome the enemy. I just mentioned a few. Christians always need strategies in place when facing spiritual warfare. Awareness is the key for success. Let this book be a guide to defeat the enemy and live victorious.

Prayer for Salvation

If you are not a Christian and would like to have power, love, and sound mind. In order to have happiness, that will lead to peace in your heart, I would like you to pray the following prayer.

Dear God:

I come before you a sinner. Thank you for sending your son Jesus Christ who died for me, and destroyed the power of death over my life. I accept Jesus now as my personal Savior and Lord, and forgive me of my sins. I choose life and to have my mind renewed in the life of Jesus.

You said that if I would confess with my mouth the Lord Jesus and believe in my heart that You raised Him from the dead, then I would be saved. I do that now. So I thank you for accepting me in the family of Christ and that I am your child. Amen.

Once you prayed that prayer, find a Bible teaching church, so that you can mature in the things of God.

The Bible is a book of seeds to the sower.
What are you believing God for?

Finances

Wealth and riches shall be in his house: and his righteousness endureth forever.(Psalms112:3)

.....the wealth of the sinner [finds its way eventually] into the hands of the righteous, for whom it was laid up. (Proverbs13:22 Amplified Bible)

But my God shall supply all your needs to His riches in glory in Christ Jesus. (Philippians 4:19)

Peace

The Lord will bless His people with peace.(Psalms29:11) When a man's ways please the Lord. He makes even his enemy to be at peace with Him. (Proverbs16:7)

And the peace of God, which passeth all understanding, shall keep your hearts and mind through Christ Jesus. (Philippians 4:7)

Patience

Knowing this, that the trying of your faith worketh patience,

but let patience have her perfect work that ye may be perfect and entire, wanting nothing. (James 1:3-4)

And let us not be weary in well doing: for in due season we shall reap, if we faint not. (Galatians 6:9)

For ye have need of patience, that, after ye have done the will of God, ye might receive the promise. (Hebrews 10:36)

Faith

So then faith comes by hearing, and hearing by the Word of God. (Romans 10:17)

Now faith is the substance of things hoped for, the evidence of things not seen. (Hebrews 11:1)

For we walk by faith, not by sight. (1Corinthains 5:7)

Worry

Thou wilt keep him in perfect peace, whose mind is stayed on thee, because he trust in thee. (Isiah 26:3)

Cast thy burden upon the lord, and He shall sustain thee. (Psalms 55:22)

The Lord also will be a refuge for the oppressed, a refuge in time of trouble. And they that know thy name will put their trust in thee: for thou, Lord hast not forsaken them that seek thee. (Psalms9:9-10)

Favor

For thou, Lord wilt bless the righteous with favor. (Psalms 5:12)

His favor is for a lifetime.......(Psalms 30:5)

For whoever finds me(wisdom) finds life and receives favor from the Lord. (Proverbs 8:35)

Wisdom

If any of you lack wisdom, let him ask of God that giveth to all liberally and upbraideth not and it shall be given him.

(James 1:5)

Behold, thou desirest truth in the inward parts: and in the hidden part thou shalt make me to know wisdom. (Psalms 51:6)

For God giveth to a man that is good in his sight wisdom, and knowledge, and joy.....(Ecclesiates 2:26)

Prayer

I urge you, first of all, to pray for all people, ask God to help them, intercede on their behalf, and give thanks for the. (1Timothy 2:1 New Living Translation Bible)

And all things, whatsoever ye shall ask in prayer, believing, ye shall receive. (Matthew 21:22)

And this is the confidence that we have in Him that if we ask anything according to his will, he heareth us: And if we know that he hears us, whatsoever we ask we know that we have the petitions that we desired of Him.(1John 5:14-15)

Fear

For I the Lord thy God will hold thy right hand saying unto thee, fear not, I will help thee.(Isaiah 41:13)

For God hath not given us the spirit of fear, but of power, and of love, and of a sound mind. (2 Timothy 1:7)

So that we may boldly say, the Lord is my helper, and I will not fear what man shall do unto me. (Hebrews 13:6)

Comfort

Though I walk in the midst of trouble, thou wilt revive me: thou shalt stretch forth thine hand against the wrath of mine enemies, and thy right hand shall save me. (Psalms 18:2).

Come unto me, all ye that labor and are heavy laden, and I will give your rest. (Matthew 11:28)

Wait on the Lord: be of good courage, and he shall strengthen thine heart: wait I say on the Lord. (Psalms 27:14)

Plant these seeds in good soil(heart) and see your harvest come to pass.
May God Bless You...........

CPSIA information can be obtained
at www.ICGtesting.com
Printed in the USA
LVOW12s1411220716
497307LV00001B/21/P